W9-DCF-018

Start TO Finish
Second Series

Everyday Products

FROM Cotton TO T-Shirt

● ROBIN NELSON

LERNER PUBLICATIONS COMPANY › Minneapolis

Lerner Publications Company
A division of Lerner Publishing Group, Inc.
241 First Avenue North
Minneapolis, MN 55401 U.S.A.

Website address: www.lernerbooks.com

Photo Acknowledgments
The images in this book are used with the permission of: © Casadphoto/Dreamstime.com, p. 1; © iStockphoto.com/kali9, p. 3; National Cotton Council, pp. 5, 7, 9; Scott Bauer/Agricultural Research Service/USDA, p. 11; © Gary Ombler/Dorling Kindersley/Getty Images, p. 13; © Cheryl Chan/Flickr/Getty Images, p. 15; © Bloomberg/Getty Images, p. 17; © AFP/Stringer/Getty Images, p. 19; © David Touchtone/Dreamstime.com, p. 21; © iStockphoto.com/mandygodbehear, p. 23.

Front cover: © Walter Arce/Dreamstime.com.

Main body text set in Arta Std Book 20/26.
Typeface provided by International Typeface Corp.

Library of Congress Cataloging-in-Publication Data

Nelson, Robin, 1971–
    From cotton to T-shirt / by Robin Nelson.
        p.   cm. — (Start to finish, second series. Everyday products)
    Audience: Grades K to 3.
    Includes index.
    ISBN 978–0–7613–6561–7 (lib. bdg. : alk. paper)
    1. T-shirts—Juvenile literature. 2. Cotton manufacture—Juvenile literature. I. Title.
    TT675.N45 2013
    646.4'35—dc23   2012007914

Manufactured in the United States of America
1 – MG – 12/31/12

TABLE OF Contents

My T-shirt keeps me cool. How was it made?

A farmer grows cotton.

T-shirts are made of cotton. Cotton comes from a plant. Cotton plants grow flowers. These flowers turn into cotton **bolls**. Each boll holds many seeds and bits of cotton.

Machines pick the cotton.

Cotton is ready to be picked in the fall. The cotton is white and fluffy. Large picking machines pick the cotton from the plants.

The cotton is cleaned.

The cotton is sent through a **cotton gin**. A cotton gin is a machine that pulls the seeds out of the cotton. The cotton gin also cleans and dries the cotton. The clean cotton is sent to a cotton mill to be made into cloth.

A machine spins the cotton.

A machine combs the cotton until it is long and thin. Then another machine spins the cotton into thin ropes called **thread**.

The thread is made into cloth.

Many spools of thread are put on a **knitting machine**. Long needles make loops and knots with the thread. The thread is knitted into cloth.

The cloth is dyed.

Cotton cloth can be dyed any color of the rainbow. Workers dip the cloth in liquid to change its color. Then the cloth is loaded onto a truck and sent to a place where T-shirts are made.

The cloth is cut.

A machine cuts the cloth into pieces. Each piece will become part of a T-shirt. The pieces are cut in many sizes for different sizes of people.

A worker sews the cloth.

A worker uses a sewing machine to sew the pieces together. They become a T-shirt.

The T-shirts are sent to stores.

The T-shirts are loaded onto trucks. The trucks take the T-shirts to stores to be sold.

I wear my T-shirt.

My soft T-shirt started as part of a plant.
It has gone from cotton to T-shirt!

23

Glossary

bolls (BOHLZ): round parts of a cotton plant that hold cotton and seeds

cotton gin (KAH-tuhn JIHN): a machine that pulls seeds out of cotton

dyed (DYD): made a different color

knitting machine (NIH-ting muh-SHEEN): a machine that makes thread into cloth

thread (THREHD): a long, thin rope made of cotton